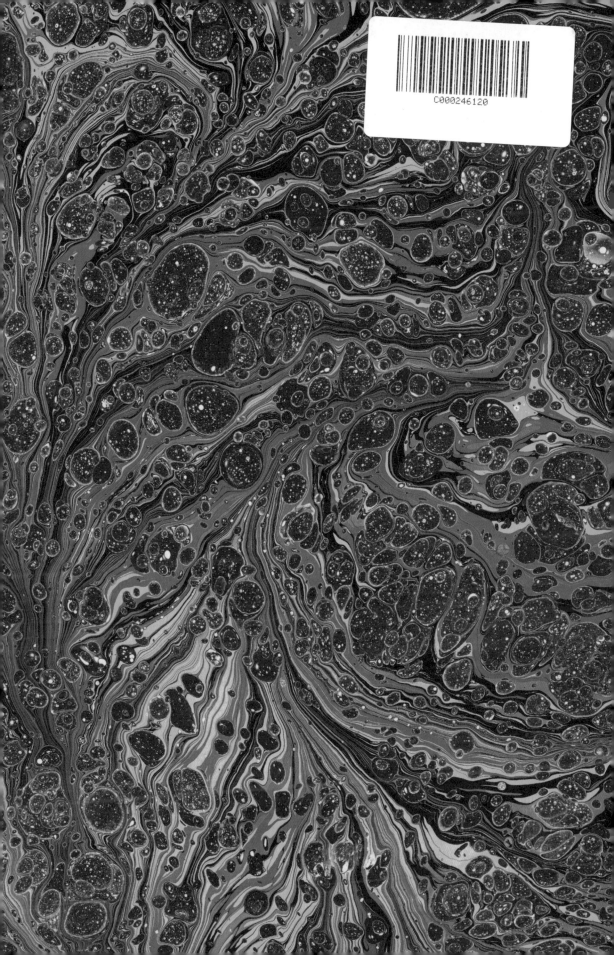

CLOSE COMBAT CLASPS
OF THE GERMAN ARMY
IN WORLD WAR II

Rolf Michaelis

Schiffer Military History
Atglen, PA

Translation from the German by Dr. Edward Force.

Book Design by Stephanie Daugherty.

Copyright © 2012 by Schiffer Publishing.
Library of Congress Control Number: 2012942402

Printed in China.
ISBN: 978-0-7643-4258-5

This book was originally published in German under the title
Das Bandenkampf-abzeichen by Michaelis-Verlag.

We are interested in hearing from authors with book ideas on related topics.

Published by Schiffer Publishing Ltd.
4880 Lower Valley Road
Atglen, PA 19310
Phone: (610) 593-1777
FAX: (610) 593-2002
E-mail: Info@schifferbooks.com.
Visit our web site at: www.schifferbooks.com
Please write for a free catalog.
This book may be purchased from the publisher.
Try your bookstore first.

In Europe, Schiffer books are distributed by:
Bushwood Books
6 Marksbury Avenue
Kew Gardens
Surrey TW9 4JF, England
Phone: 44 (0) 20 8392-8585
FAX: 44 (0) 20 8392-9876
E-mail: Info@bushwoodbooks.co.uk.
Visit our website at: www.bushwoodbooks.co.uk

Contents

FOREWORD

When Hitler created the Close Combat Clasp at the end of 1942, the course of the war was already beginning to change, and not in favor of Germany. The battles were hard and costly; more and more, the Allies took over the law of action. While the Assault Badge was given for storming ahead, the Close Combat Clasp took more and more days into account in which, because of the developing situation, the enemy soldiers who broke into the German positions had to be driven back in close combat.

Close combat meant "hand-to-hand" fighting for the soldiers. Practically every soldier was wounded at least once in this combat; countless lives were lost. The total of only about 600 awards of the Close Combat Clasp in Gold speaks for itself. For many men, the survival of close combat meant a great spiritual burden after the war ended. The reader of this volume might keep that in mind.

Rolf Michaelis
Erlangen, August 1996

INTRODUCTION

Operation "Barbarossa", the war with the Soviet Union, brought changes to the European theater of war in various ways. While the German Wehrmacht was able to defeat and occupy the opposing countries – except Britain – in just a few weeks, this ended in the USSR, what with the vastness of the land, the climatic conditions, and the almost inexhaustible manpower that was available to the Red Army. The battles, often lasting for weeks and months (German summer and Russian winter offensives), with the resulting number of combats, never attained in the previous short campaigns, resulted in new decorations being created gradually.

Thus Adolf Hitler, on November 25, 1942, after some seventeen months of the eastern campaign and thirty-eight months of waging war in his capacity as Fuehrer of the German Reich and Commander-in-chief of the Army, created the Close Combat Clasp:

> "… as a visible sign of recognition the soldiers fighting man against man with bare weapons and close-combat weapons, but at the same time as an impetus to the highest fulfillment of duty."

"The impetus to the highest fulfillment of duty" was for Hitler presumably the decisive feature. By the end of 1942 the German Wehrmacht had already had to survive several severe crises in the Russian campaign, in which Hitler had given "hold-on orders" (meaning, do not retreat one step) again and again. It is only natural that with combat conducted in that way, the confrontation of the two war parties led to the hardest fighting – along with countless close combats.

Every soldier of the German Wehrmacht and the units subordinated to it (such as the Waffen-SS) who got into battle unprotected and on foot could be awarded the Close Combat Clasp. Most of them were grenadiers. Foreigners also received the medals. Prominent bearers of the Close Combat Clasp in Gold included, for example, the Belgian Walloon leader and Commander of the 28th SS Volunteer Grenadier Division "Wallonien", Leon Degrelle. Awards to members of a foreign armed force, even those allied with the German Reich, such as those of Slovakia, were forbidden.

Award envelope for the Close Combat Clasp in Silver.

Award envelope for the Close Combat Clasp in Gold.

Since the Close Combat Clasp, as its name already suggests, was given in honor of close combat, *"man against man,"* the awarding of the Army's Assault Badge was kept separate from it, even when the assault, the breaking into enemy positions, led to close combat. In that case the day was called an assault and close combat day.

The following report shows that in town fighting in particular, constant close combat resulted from repeating attacks and counterattacks. Especially noteworthy was February 8, 1944, on which *"hours-long stubborn close combat"* was recorded (KTB Rgt.Ger.258):

> Combat Report from the battle days in Kwitki from 2/1-8/44
> For 2/1/44 the *Rgt.Gr.* was ordered to continue the attack on Kwitki. At 11:00 A.M. the *Rgt.Gr.* advanced with the following structure:
>
> 11.Kp. (Kp. Lehnart) as strongest Kp. As attack spearhead, 9.Kp. in right rear position, 10.Kp. as reserve behind the staff. At 12:15 P.M. the first attack goal, the highland 1.5 km south of Petruski, was reached without enemy contact. From this highland a straight stretch 800 meters long led to the ditch north of Kwitki. Through observation the town was seen to be strongly occupied by the enemy. At 4:00 P.M. the further attack was begun. At this time it was already so dark that the possibility of moving the strong enemy weapons was taken. For this attack the Regiment Group was reorganized, and the 9.Kp. was on the right, 11.Kp. in the middle, 7./258 on the left.
>
> The open space was partly taken in one jump, and after a short hard fight (the enemy was completely surprised and noticed the attack over the open space too late) the 11.Kp. advanced into the northern houses of Kwitki. A renewed advance at 11:00 P.M. along the village street brought the ditch that ran from Kwitki-North to the northwest into our possession. An enemy counterstroke was beaten off bloodily for them.
>
> [2.2] During the last night the enemy strengthened itself particularly with heavy weapons and fired at us all day with artillery, antitank guns and grenade launchers. With grenade launchers they made firefalls up to 200 shots. With Pak they fired on every individual man, the infantry used, for the most part, explosive and particularly incendiary bullets, with which they

Confirmation in a *soldbuch* of the awarding of the Close Combat Clasp in Bronze.

set fire to the thatched houses. The command post of the 11.Kp. had to be moved several times. After night fell the 11.Kp. made another attack to improve its own positions. It was able to move its positions 200 meters forward by this attack. The enemy then made three or four counterattacks, all of which were driven off.

[2.3.] All movement on our side immediately brought on very heavy enemy fire. At 5:30 P.M. the Russians fired a very heavy grenade-launcher firefall of 200 to 300 shots on the northern part of Kwitki and then made an attack against the Strohschober heights. This was occupied only by two groups of the 9.Kp. Through their superior power the Russians were able to take possession of the Strohschober heights. At the same time they made another firefall on the northern part of Kwitki that apparently was meant to make a counterstroke by us impossible. The Staff and company Troop of the 12.Kp. immediately made a counterattack, picked up the scattered groups of the 9.Kp. and regained possession of the Strohschober heights in brief close combat with loud cheering. A group advanced by the 11.Kp. for possible support was not needed. A Russian counterattack late in the evening led to breaking into the positions of the 11.Kp. Here too, the enemy was immediately driven back by a counterthrust. Ten enemy dead were counted.

[2.4.] For February 4 the taking of the town of Kwitki was ordered. At 5:00 A.M. the Regiment Group began the attack on the Windmill heights and was able, with good artillery support, to report the occupation of the Windmill heights. An immediate enemy counterthrust, supported by a tank, was driven off by the 9.Kp. The attack of the 11.Kp. along the village street to the southwest gained no ground, since the flank fire especially the concentrated fire of the enemy's heavy weapons was too strong. Another attack of the 9th and 11th Companies at 10:00 A.M. also gained no success. The enemy fired with unheard-of ammunition supplies. At 2:00 P.M. the Regiment Group advanced again, but in a few meters was stopped by a hail of enemy artillery and grenade-launcher fire. The attack on Kwitki was then ordered halted and defensive action was resumed.

[2.5.] During the whole night the Russians fire heavy grenade-launcher fire, especially in the sector of the 11.Kp. By day too, the enemy fire did not let up. After night fell the enemy made

Willi Rogmann

a strong advance against the sector of the 11.Kp., but it was driven off.

[2.6.] On this day there was often grenade-launcher fire and heavy rifle and machine-gun fire. Otherwise the day passed more quietly than the days before.

[2.7.] About 1:00 A.M. the Russians fired two heavy grenade-launcher firefalls, especially on the sector of the 11.Kp.

[2.8.] At 1:10 A.M. there was another heavy enemy firefall on the sector of the 11.Kp. and Kwitki-North. At the same time the enemy began to attack and broke into the positions of the 11.Kp. Only at 6:00 A.M. could the old situation – after hours of stubborn close combat – be re-established by an energetic counterthrust. At 10:25 A.M.
A salvo firefall was made on the 9.Kp. It caused no losses. After night fell the Russians again attacked the sector of the 11.Kp., but it was driven off.
[2.9.] About 12:00 noon came the order to retake the heights north of Kwitki after nightfall. At 7:30 P.M. the Russians attacked the positions of the 11.Kp. again. They were able to break into the positions. Only by a counterthrust could they be thrown out. The removal of the enemy delayed us until 11:00 P.M. The last parts of the 11.Kp. with Lt. Lehnart, who was already nicknamed *"the Lion of Kwitki"*, left the northern part of Kwitki at 11:15 P.M. and moved into their new battle line unnoticed by the enemy."

Every day from December 1, 1942 could be called a close-combat day, which gave the soldiers the opportunity to have seen "the whites of the enemy's eyes". It was not important whether this occurred in an attack, in defense, or, for example, in a scouting-troop action. In the same way, there was at first no determination of the location of the close combat. This could take place on the front or in the hinterlands. After the creation of the Anti-Partisan Badge on January 30, 1944 there came the Close Combat Clasp of August 21, 1944, but only to be awarded for action at the front against regular forces.

The former *SS-Oberscharführer* Willi Rogmann (7./SS Panzergrenadier Regiment 2) recalls a close-combat day:

"At the beginning we moved forward wrapped in a line of riflemen. We did this although the ground before us had not been scouted. In the dark of night, with no moonlight, we slipped up the mountain (2000 meters), All was still. Not a sound was heard. We were not allowed to talk and were to avoid any sound, so as not to warn the enemy. They let us come on about 30 meters and then smeared us with fire from all their guns. The chief was not up front with us, but had waited in Vevi for our report of success. So we withdrew on orders from our own platoon leaders. Dead and wounded were brought back with us. The withdrawal led to vigorous accusations from our chief when we reached him in back. But now nothing more was to be done anyway, and why wasn't he up front with us, like Gerd Pleiss, the Chief of the 1st Company? On the next day our artillery, since it would no longer be a surprise attack, was to shoot till the enemy was ready to be stormed. But that too was a flop, at least in our sector. All of two shells from the 10.5 cm light field artillery flew over us and away. That was the whole artillery preparation. Without hope for further support, we climbed back up the mountains. Below the vegetation border they were overgrown with thick shrubs, so that we had good cover, at least at the beginning. But nobody fired at us. We believed the enemy positions had meanwhile been deserted, until the shrubbery grew shorter and the cover worse. When we came within 50 meters of the positions, the firing started up again. We now lay as if on a platter, and it was clear that if we retreated now, they would shoot us down to the last man. But we didn't actually think such a thing, for we could have escaped, we would be chased higher up until the domineering heights were taken. So we made the jump until we were standing right in front of our enemies. Like the other riflemen, I had drawn my side arm and jumped to a rifle trench. Then my enemy straightened up. In his shallow hole he was almost exactly as big as I was when I stood outside. Since he did not raise his hands, but hit at me with his pistol, I rammed my side arm into his abdomen, as we had been taught in training, turned it and kicked toward him. Naturally he now collapsed and turned his eyes away. To me the situation was disgusting, but I had no time to think about it, for my group leader Latter had ordered his opponent to surrender. Then the latter shot him through the hand. Latter went wild and roared that I should also ram my side arm into him. But I preferred to shoot him with a 'Deutschuss', as they call it when the rifle is not properly aimed. The others raised their hands, and the fight was fortunately over. They were driven together and taken away at once. But we first searched for the food that they had left behind. We wanted for once to be supplied as well as they were. Our smokers stuck the first Plaiers Medium between their teeth. I myself, who was always hungry, opened a can of corned beef and ate the uncommon box of white bread along with it."

Since, as one can tell by the narratives above, storming an enemy position often involved close combat, the three days evaluated as assault days would be regarded as close combat days for the Assault Badge awarded as of July 1, 1942. Limited by the relatively late creation and the course of the war that turned against Germany as of 1943, the fighting off of enemy breakthroughs into German positions resulted in the must close combat.

With the day of awarding, there also came the possibility that in unbroken action on the eastern front with the extent of the following could be calculated:

15 months   up to 15 close combat days

12 months   up to 10 close combat days

8 months   up to 5 close combat days

The conscientious checking of these conditions was to be done by the unit leader.

The company leaders were supposed to tell their superior battalion or regimental commanders, in their daily reports, which days had led to close combat. The latter then decided whether the day's action could be evaluated as a day of close combat. Every soldier was to carry a form in his *soldbuch* on which the company leader designated the close combat days. Beyond that, the company leaders provided additional lists of names and added them to the war diary.

Qualified for awarding were the commanders of independent battalions an on upward. For wounded men, before the required number of close combat days, awarding could be undertaken only by a superior officer with the rank of a division commander. As for men killed in action or accidents, there was the possibility of posthumous awarding when the conditions were met by the day of death at the latest. The Close Combat Clasp was then to be sent to the dead man's next of kin along with the certificate of possession.

As opposed to the assault badge, which the responsible regimental commander could also award to prisoners of war or internees, or missing soldiers, this was not possible for the Close Combat Clasp. Here the soldier lost the eligibility for an award.

The artistic design of the Close Combat Clasp was made by graphic artist Wilhelm E. Peekhaus. In the middle of the design the two close combat weapons – sidearm and stick grenade – were crossed under the Wehrmacht eagle and framed at left and right as well as below by small oak leaves. At the left and right sides of the medal were larger oak leaves, along with rays. The medals were originally made out of so-called non-ferrous metal, later of fine zinc, and bronzed, silvered or gilded. The middle part around the eagle, sidearm and bayonet was pierced and fitted with a steel-blue to black metal back plate. This was practically the only German badge that was produced in that way. Neither the Assault Badge nor, for example, the Luftwaffe badges, all of which were pierced, had a metal back plate. Only in 1945 was this laborious production form dropped – the medal was no longer pierced – the plates already pressed on. On the back, the needle was horizontal, with which the Close Combat Clasp was fastened above the left breast pocket, or over the ribbon clasp (of non-wearable decorations).

THE CLOSE COMBAT CLASP IN BRONZE

The requirement for awarding the first level of the Close Combat Clasp – the Close Combat Clasp in Bronze – was usually fifteen days of close combat. Since fifteen close combat days could be calculated for unbroken action of fifteen months on the eastern front, it was possible that the first bronze badges were awarded as early as December 1942. For wounded men, who because of their wound or damage were no longer in a situation to receive the Close Combat Clasp, they could be awarded if their action had justified it up to that time, and the man could prove at least ten close combat days. The awarding of the Close Combat Clasp in Bronze generally also justified the possession of the Iron Cross Second Class.

THE CLOSE COMBAT CLASP IN SILVER

The Close Combat Clasp in Silver could be given after thirty close combat days, as a rule. If the soldier was wounded and thus could no longer take part in close combat from then on, it was possible to award him the silver level as long as he could prove twenty close combat days. The awarding of the Iron Cross First Class was justified at the latest with the awarding of the Close Combat Clasp in Silver. Hitler ordered this when he learned at the first ceremonial awarding of the golden Close Combat Clasp on August 27, 1944 that an *Unteroffizier* had not yet been awarded the E.K.I.

THE CLOSE COMBAT CLASP IN GOLD

The Close Combat Clasp in Gold, as a rule, was awarded for fifty documented close combat days. If the soldier was wounded so that he could not take part in any more close combat days, then he had to have at least forty close combat days attested to be able to be awarded the highest level of the medal. The first awardings of the Close Combat Clasp in Gold took place in the latter half of 1943.

On April 8, 1944, Hitler declared that he wanted to award the highest infantry medal, as he designated the Close Combat Clasp in Gold, personally from then on. That did not mean that he conferred them. For that, the appropriate commanders were to submit a report of the awarding to the Army Personnel Office.

For the first awarding of the third level by Hitler on August 27, 1944 at his field headquarters, special badges with award containers were produced. Unlike most of the badges, which were made only of fine zinc or pressed hollow at the end of the war, the more valuable, so-called non-ferrous metal, was used once again. The Close Combat Clasps were fire-gilded and the edges polished. Probably caused by the fire-gilding, the metal plate was not attached like the simple badges, but by a rivet and a small hook on the back. This version was always made without a manufacturer's trademark. The containers were lengthy, as were the badges. The upper and lower parts of the containers were made of black paper outside, while the inside of the envelope was lined with satin cloth above and black velour below in which the Close Combat Clasp could be placed.

Without further justification, the third level of the Close Combat Clasp was to justify the awarding of the German Cross in Gold, since the earning of it was linked with very special bravery and enterprise. Besides that, the recipients also received at first fourteen and later twenty-one days of special furlough, and were to be released from front service for a year, so that they could pass on their experience to the recruits in the replacement units.

The number of awarded Close Combat Clasps in gold was approximately 600. About 100 of them were awarded to members of the Waffen-SS:

- ca. 20% of the Close Combat Clasp in Gold went to enlisted men

- ca. 55% of the Close Combat Clasp in Gold went to non-commissioned officers

- ca. 25% of the Close Combat Clasp in Gold went to officers.

The then *SS-Oberscharführer* Willi Rogmann recalls the presentation of the Close Combat Clasp in Gold:

> "I had far more than 100 close combat days, of which 68 were calculated, since they were counted only as of 1942. In my case the awarding was done on June 2, 1944 by my regimental commander, *SS-Obersturmbannführer* Rudolf Sandig, who did not actually have the right to confer it. This belonged to Hitler or a deputy named by him.
>
> On July 18, 1944 I was wounded for the eighth time and finally went to ambulant treatment at the Helmstedt reserve hospital. There I received a telegram that I was to report instantly to the Wehrmacht Adjutancy in the Reich Chancellery. Since they had no Waffen-SS uniforms at the hospital and my uniform had been torn when I was wounded, I went to Berlin in the mended uniform of a Wehrmacht *Unteroffizier*. At the Reich Chancellery *Oberstleutnant* von Amsberg, as the appropriate adjutant, received me. He had summoned me and two comrades from my battalion to him for conferring of the medal by Hitler at the Wolf's Lair. We were to travel to East Prussia on a courier train. It was to be the second conferring by Hitler on September 5, 1944. Amsberg asked me if I knew where my two comrades were, whom he had also summoned. But Gerhard Bauer had already died at my side on July 7, 1944 in the defense of the bridgehead at Sereth. Siegfried Friedhoff was in the Falaise pocket in Normandy at that time and could not come either.
>
> Well, said Herr von Amsberg, and you cannot come into this elevator wearing a mended Wehrmacht uniform. So we shall postpone the event. Give me your regular location, so I can reach you when it is time. And get a respectable uniform by

then. When I explained that at the time I was in hospital, but did not know for how long, Herr von Amsberg wrote me a furlough form until called. When I was to be released from the hospital, I was to go home and wait until he called me.

Well, I had never before seen such a furlough form, much less the many depot guards whom I excited with it in the next few months. On December 10, 1944 I again received a telegram, according to which I was to be in the city hall chamber in Ulm on the morning of December 12 to be awarded the Close Combat Clasp by the *Reichsführer-SS*. I still did not have a better uniform. Naturally, I, unlike Hitler, who had himself been a simple soldier in World War I, would never have dared to stand before Himmler in such a shabby uniform. That could have had consequences. By chance I met an *Unterscharführer* of the "Das Reich" Division who was on furlough and could lend me his field blouse for my purpose.

On the morning of December 12 all the expected soldiers me in the city hall chamber in Ulm. Himmler came and gave a speech, as if we were just short of the final victory. Then he handed the medals to us individually with a few words – as Hitler's deputy. Afterward he invited us to a midday meal together at the Ratskeller there. Himmler wanted to have me and my friend Siegfried Friedhoff at his table for eight. When Himmler wanted to talk with us, everybody at the table kept his mouth tightly closed, for such talking was dangerous. Only Siegfried told Himmler the truth, and I could have sunk into the ground. My friend had never shown signs of anxiety, but here, in my opinion, it would have been better to keep quiet. *SS-Obersturmbannführer* Grothmann, Himmler's adjutant, wrote furlough forms for us after the dinner. Each of us received 21 days of special leave. I myself could find out where I was going from the recovery company. There was no longer much of a choice, so I went to the Guard Battalion in Berlin. I would like to mention that we received the same honors, by the Führer's orders, as the Knight's Cross holders. For me that looked as if every month a big package with things to enjoy would reach my members."

The Close Combat Clasp in Bronze.

The Close Combat Clasp in Silver.

The Close Combat Clasp in Gold.

Two clasps made by C.E. Juncker in Berlin.

Two clasps made by Friedrich Linden in Luedenscheid.

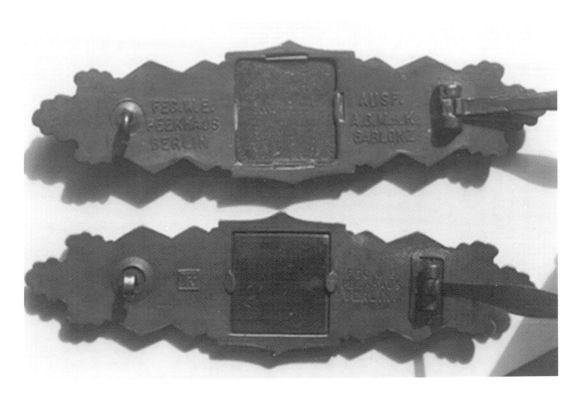

Upper clasp: Clasp and Plastic Work Group, Gablonz.

Lower clasp: Josef Feix's Söhne, Gablonz.

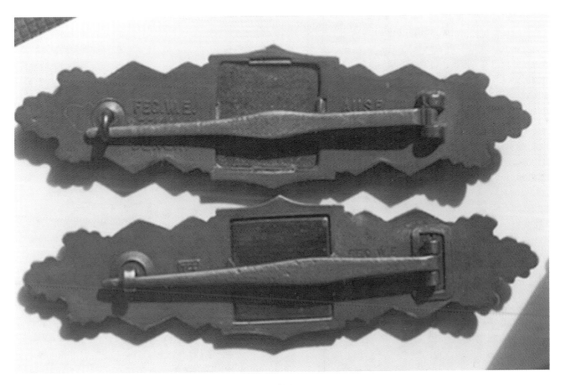

Two more clasps from the A.G.M.u.K., Gablonz with smaller manufacturer's trademarks and varying pin system and plate fastenings.

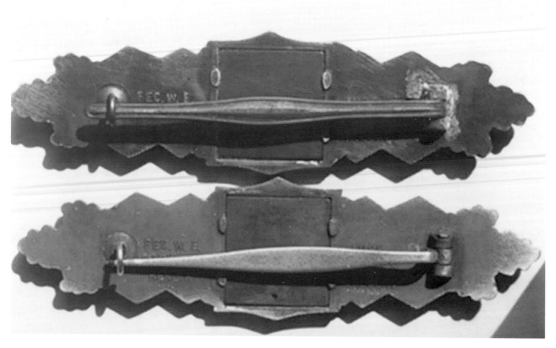

Detail close-ups.

**Helmut *Ritter* von Traitteur was awarded the Close Combat Clasp
in Bronze and the German Cross in Gold on June 1, 1944.**

ins Soldbuch eintragen lassen! 5.

B e s i t z z e u g n i s .
==

Dem S t a b s g e f r e i t e n

Paul G r u n d m a n n

4./ Pz.Aufkl.Abt. 26

verleihe ich für tapfere Teilnahme an
15 Nahkampftagen

die 1. Stufe der
Nahkampfspange.

Abt.Gef.Std., 20.4.1944.

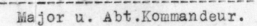

—————————————————————————————————
Major u. Abt.Kommandeur.

A front-prepared possession certificate for the first level of the Close Combat Clasp.

BESITZZEUGNIS

DEM .... Obergefreiten ....
(DIENSTGRAD)

.... Kurt M i l e w s k i ....
(VOR- UND FAMILIENNAME)

.... Frontaufklärungskommando 202 ....
(TRUPPENTEIL)
- Einheit "Schill" -

VERLEIHE ICH FÜR TAPFERE TEILNAHME

AN 15 NAHKAMPFTAGEN

DIE 1. STUFE DER
NAHKAMPFSPANGE

O.U., den 25. Febr. 1945
(ORT UND DATUM)
Für das Obkdo.d.Heeresgruppe Mitte
Der Chef des Generalstabes
I A
(UNTERSCHRIFT)

(STEMPEL)

Oberstleutnant i.G.
(DIENSTGRAD UND DIENSTSTELLUNG)

This Close Combat Clasp was awarded for action in the defeat of the Slova national revolt.

32

Besitzzeugnis

Dem _____ Stabsfeld-ebel
Dienstgrad

Otto P i n k o w
Vor- und Familienname

4. / Gren.Rgt. 376
Truppenteil

verleihe ich für tapfere Teilnahme an   15   Nahkampftagen

die   1.   Stufe der

Nahkampfspange

Rgts.Gef.Std.,den 10.11.44
Ort und Datum

_____
Unterschrift

Major u. Rgts.-Führer
Dienstgrad und Dienststellung

Wehrkreisdruckerei X Hamburg 13

An interesting variation of a possession certificate.

33

BESITZZEUGNIS

DEM   Gefreiten

(DIENSTGRAD)

Fritz S c h r ö d e r

(VOR. UND FAMILIENNAME)

3./Grenadier-Regiment 101

(TRUPPENTEIL)

VERLEIHE ICH FÜR TAPFERE TEILNAHME

AN 15 NAHKAMPFTAGEN

DIE 1. STUFE DER
NAHKAMPFSPANGE

Rgt.Gef.St., 3. November 1944

(ORT UND DATUM)

(STEMPEL)   (UNTERSCHRIFT)

Major und Regimentsführer.

(DIENSTGRAD UND DIENSTSTELLUNG)

Gefreite Schroeder was awarded the first and second levels

of the Close Combat Clasp on the same day.

BESITZZEUGNIS

DEM   Gefreiten
                       (DIENSTGRAD)

Fritz S c h r ö d e r
(VOR- UND FAMILIENNAME)

3./Grenadier-Regiment 101
(TRUPPENTEIL)

VERLEIHE ICH FÜR TAPFERE TEILNAHME
AN 30 NAHKAMPFTAGEN

DIE 2 . STUFE DER
NAHKAMPFSPANGE

Rgt.Gef.St., 3. November 1944
(ORT UND DATUM)

(STEMPEL)   (UNTERSCHRIFT)

Major und Regimentsführer.
(DIENSTGRAD UND DIENSTSTELLUNG)

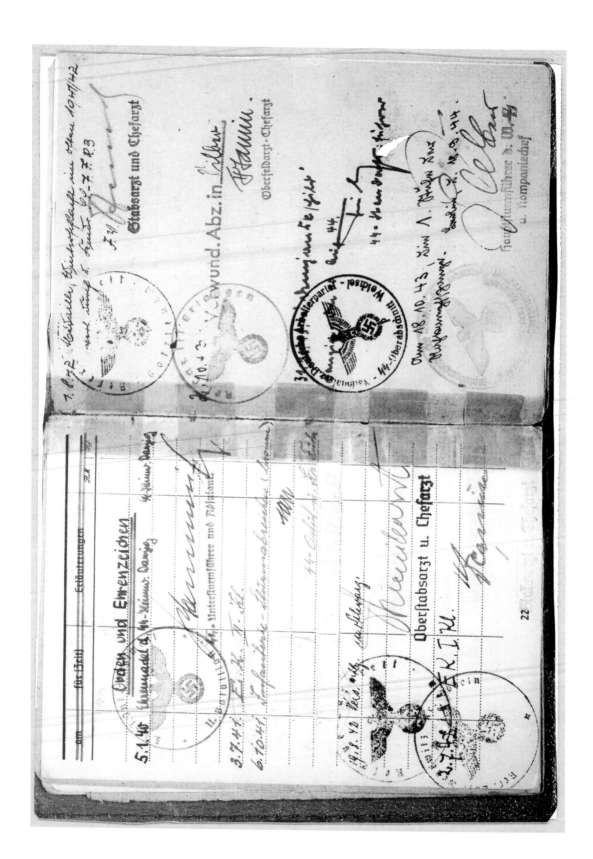

Stabsarzt und Chefarzt

V. Sch. wund. Abz. in ...

Oberfeldarzt · Chefarzt

Hauptsturmführer d. W.-SS
u. Kompaniechef

Orden und Ehrenzeichen

am	für (Zeit)	Erläuterungen	F.K.

5.1.40   Ehrennadel d. N.-Kleinz. Danzig

3.7.41   E.K. II. Kl.

6.10.41 Infanterie-Sturmabzeichen (Bronze)

Oberstabsarzt u. Chefarzt

22 ...arzt · Chefarzt

Willi Rogmann

BESITZZEUGNIS

DEM   ᛋᛋ-Unterscharführer
(DIENSTGRAD)

Willi Rogmann
(VOR. UND FAMILIENNAME)

1M/AH / 7. / 2.Panz.Gren.Rgt.
(TRUPPENTEIL)

VERLEIHE ICH FÜR TAPFERE TEILNAHME

AN _15_ NAHKAMPFTAGEN

DIE _1_. STUFE DER

NAHKAMPFSPANGE

Rgts.Gef.St., den 1.9.1943
(ORT UND DATUM)

(STEMPEL)

(UNTERSCHRIFT)

ᛋᛋ-Obersturmbannführer u.
Rgt.-Kommandeur
(DIENSTGRAD UND DIENSTSTELLUNG)

**Possession certificate for the later bearer
of the Close Combat Clasp in Gold, Willi Rogmann.**

1.SS-Panzer Division
"Leibstandarte SS Adolf Hitler"
SS-Panzer-Grenadier-Regiment 2

Reichsführer-SS Persönl. St.
Verb. Off. b. OKH / PA /D 5
Eingang 24. Jan. 1945
Tgb. Nr 142 / 45 Ra

542

Vorschlag Nr. 87
für die Verleihung des
Deutschen Kreuzes in Gold

Träger der _____ _____

_____

Verliehen: 8. 2. 45

Rgts.Gef.Std. den 15. 12. 1944

(Unterschrift)
SS-Obersturmbannführer
und Rgts.-Kommandeur

(Dienstgrad und Dienststellung)

The holding of the Close Combat Clasp in Gold justified
the awarding of the German Cross in Gold.

Fünfzigmal Sieger im Nahkampf geblieben

Reichsführer ﬆ Heinrich Himmler überreichte 81 Soldaten die Nahkampfspange in Gold

Berlin, 14. Dez.

Im Auftrage des Führers überreichte der Befehlshaber des Ersatzheeres, Reichsführer ﬆ Heinrich Himmler, an 81 Angehörige des Heeres und der Waffen-ﬆ, die im Saal des Rathauses einer süddeutschen Stadt angetreten waren, die Nahkampfspange in Gold. Anschließend an den feierlichen Akt waren die Soldaten die Gäste des Gauleiters.

Es ist die unerschütterliche Front der am Feinde stehenden Soldaten, die die Grenzen des Reiches schützt. Unter dem Hagel der Artillerie und der Bomben harrt der Infanterist aus, um den angreifenden Feind abzuweisen; immer wieder greift er auch selbst an und bringt in kühnen Unternehmungen in die Stellungen des Gegners ein. Zur Ehrung solcher unermüdlichen Kämpfer hat der Führer die Nahkampfspange gestiftet.

Von den 81 Offizieren und Männern des Heeres, ﬆ-Führern und ﬆ-Männern, die am 12. Dezember im Saal des Rathauses angetreten waren, hat im letzten Jahr jeder einzelne dem Feinde 50mal im Nahkampf gegenübergestanden, 50mal hat er dem Tode ins Auge gesehen und 50mal ist er Sieger geblieben.

Einige Vertreter militärischer Dienststellen und Behörden sind mit diesen Männern versammelt, als der Reichsführer ﬆ den Saal betritt. Er schart die Soldaten zwanglos in einem Halbkreis um sich, er weiß, daß diese Tapfersten der Tapferen zu ihren Taten nur fähig waren, weil ihnen allen der Sinn unseres Kampfes bewußt ist. Auf das große Ziel, das uns vor Augen steht, lenkte der Reichsführer ﬆ dann auch die Gedanken der um ihn versammelten Soldaten. Er sprach davon, daß das deutsche Volk in dem nun zu Ende gehenden Jahr von harten Schicksalsschlägen heimgesucht wurde. Front und Heimat haben diese Schläge nicht nur ertragen, sondern brachten die Kräfte auf, die im Westen und Osten gleich-

zeitig eindringende Flut der Feinde zum Stehen zu bringen. Nachdem das Schwerste überstanden war, ist die Front zu neuen Kräften gekommen. „Ich kenne genau die Nöte der Front und der Heimat," sagte der Reichsführer ﬆ, „aber ich weiß auch, wie es bei unseren Feinden aussieht."

Nach einem kurzen Ueberblick über die militärische und politische Lage auf der Feindseite gab der Reichsführer ﬆ dann seiner Ueberzeugung Ausdruck, daß dieser Krieg siegreich beendet werden wird. Wie die Heimat in Standhaftigkeit und Tapferkeit unermüdlich an den neuen Waffen gearbeitet hat und arbeiten wird, so hat der Frontsoldat durch Tapferkeit und Standhaftigkeit den Feind an der Durchführung seiner Vernichtungspläne gehindert und wird ihn weiter hindern.

Der Reichsführer ﬆ erinnerte an das Wort des Führers, „Tapferkeit vollbringt Wunder", und würdigte mit diesen Worten die Leistungen der vor ihm stehenden Soldaten, die er als Spitzenauslese der deutschen Armee bezeichnete. Er übermittelte den 81 Männern den Dank des Führers und des Vaterlandes und sagte ihnen, der Führer sei davon überzeugt, daß der deutsche Soldat ebenso wie in den vergangenen Jahren auch im künftigen Jahr standhaft und tapfer kämpfen werde.

Dann wandte sich der Reichsführer ﬆ jedem einzelnen zu und überreichte im Namen des Führers die hohe Auszeichnung.

Was jeder dieser Männer, unter denen sich mancher kaum 20jährige befand, in seinem kämpferischen Leben erfahren hat, läßt sich nicht allein an den Auszeichnungen ablesen, die seine Brust zieren. Kaum einer, der nicht ein oder mehrere Male verwundet wurde. Fast die Hälfte der nun mit der hohen Auszeichnung Bedachten trug das Verwundetenabzeichen in Silber oder Gold. Fast ebenso häufig sah man das Deutsche Kreuz in Gold, während einige der Kämpfer sogar das Ritterkreuz trugen.

A newspaper clipping from the *Ulm Tageblatt* of December 14, 1944.
Five days later the city hall chamber was burned out after an Allied bomb attack.

SS-Rottenführer Georg Kachel received the
Close Combat Clasp in Gold on November 15, 1943.

BESITZZEUGNIS

DEM   ⁜ - Rottenführer ,
(DIENSTGRAD)

K a c h e l ,   Georg
(VOR- UND FAMILIENNAME)

15./⁜ Pz.Gren.Rgt. 4   " Der Führer "
(TRUPPENTEIL)

VERLEIHE ICH FÜR TAPFERE TEILNAHME

AN 5o NAHKAMPFTAGEN

DIE III. STUFE DER

NAHKAMPFSPANGE
(i. G O L D)

Rgt.Gef.Std., den 15. Nov. 1943
(ORT UND DATUM)

(UNTERSCHRIFT)

(STEMPEL)   ⁜-Obersturmbannführer u.Rgt.Kdr.
(DIENSTGRAD UND DIENSTSTELLUNG)

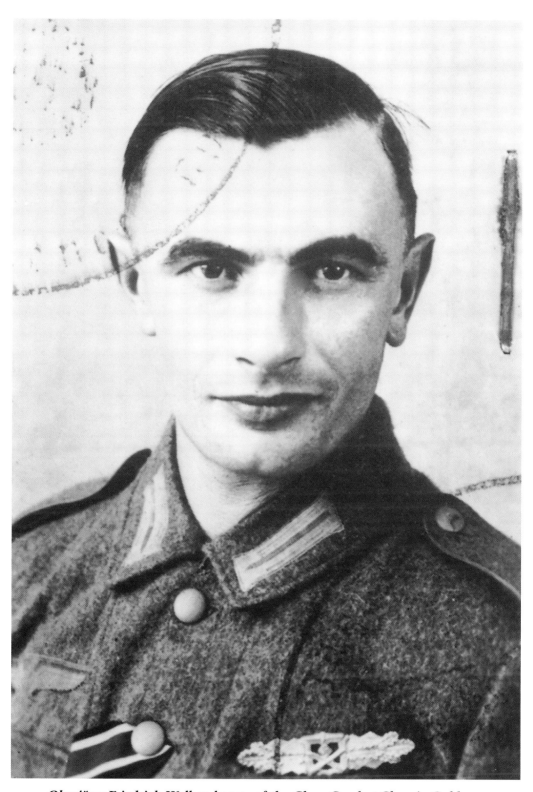

Oberjäger Friedrich Wolber, bearer of the Close Combat Clasp in Gold.

Beurlaubungen über fünf Tage
(Vor Urlaubsantritt auszufüllen)

1. Dom 9.7.44 bis 24.1.44 nach Gutach

Grund: Erh. Urlaub.

den 7. Jan. 1944

u. Unterschrift.

(Unterschrift des Komp., Truppenführers usw.)

Dienststempel

2. Dom 30.5. bis 14.6.44 nach Gutach

Grund: Erh. Urlaub.

den 14. Mai 1944

u. Unterschrift.

(Unterschrift des Komp. Truppenführers usw.)

Dienststempel

3. Dom 5.2. bis 21.2.45 nach Gutach - Turm

Freifahrt 1+2 Grund: Genesungsurlaub

den 5. 2. 1945

Friedrich

(Unterschrift des Komp., Gruppenführers usw.)

Oberleutnant u. Komp.-Führer

Dienststempel

4. Dom 22.2.45 bis 14.3.45 nach Gutach - Turm

21 Grund: Sonderurlaub Träger der Goldenen Nahkampfspange

den 5. 2. 1945

Friedrich

(Unterschrift des Komp. Truppenführers usw.)

Oberleutnant u. Komp.-Führer

Dienststempel

23

For bearers of the Close Combat Clasp in Gold,
there were twenty-one days of special furlough.

O.U., den 13.6.1945.

A n t r a g auf

Verleihung der Nahkampfspange III. Stufe.

Name:

Vorname:

Dienstgrad: SS-Hauptsturmführer

Geburtstag und -ort:

Heimatanschrift:

Letzte Einheit: SS-Pz.Gren.Btl. 5o6

Militärische Verwendung: Bataillonsführer

Verleihungsdatum der Nahkampfspange I. Stufe: 19. 3.1944
Verleihungsdatum der Nahkampfspange II.Stufe: 9.11.1944

N a h k a m p f t a g e :

1.	1. 7.41	Inf.-Werk westlich Salla/nordfinnland.
2.	17. 8.41	Spähtrupp bei km 23.
3.	18. 8.41	Angriff bei km 23.
4.	22. 8.41	Angriff Kampfgruppe Schreiber.
5.	1.11.41	Stosstrupp auf feindl. Bunkerlinien.
6.	3.11.41	Angriff bei km 14,2.
7.	8.11.41	Angriff bei km 14,5.
8.	1o.11.41	Spähtrupp auf Berg Neu-wara.
9.	12.11.41	Spähtrupp auf Berg Neu-wara.
1o.	17.11.41	Angriff auf Berg Neu-wara.
11.	17. 5.42	Angriff bei See 73.
12.	18. 5.42	Angriff bei See 75.
13.	19. 5.42	Abwehr bei Kampfgruppe Jordt.
14.	2o. 5.42	Gegenstoss bei See 75/74.
15.	22. 5.42	Abwehr bei See 73.

-2-

This Close Combat Clasp in Gold was applied for by a prisoner of war.

16.	30. 6.43	Abwehr auf Berg Bende-wara.
17.	11.10.43	Stosstruppunternehmen 1.000 m westl. Bende-wara.
18.	17. 3.44	Abwehr auf Landzunge Kapanez-See.
19.	12. 7.44	Angriff auf Mungohügel.
20.	15. 7.44	Einbruch in Stellungen auf Schneisenhöhe.
21.	17. 7.44	Angriff auf Mungohügel.
22.	12. 9.44	Abgew.Angriff zwischen 1.Kp. und Abschnitt Derflinger.
23.	14. 9.44	Feindangriff ostw. der Korjastrasse.
24.	16. 9.44	Abgew. Vorstoss ostw. km 14 der Korjastrasse.
25.	7.10.44	Verteidigung der Stadt Kemi.
26.	8.10.44	Verteidigung und Absetzung aus der Stadt Kemi.
27.	9.10.44	Spähtrupp
28.	12.10.44	Abgew. Feindangriff bei km 39 alte Mickelstrasse.
29.	13.10.44	Angriff bis km 41 alte Mickelstrasse.
30.	14.10.44	Abwehr beim km 41,4 alte Mickelstrasse.
31.	18.10.44	Abwehr bei km 35 alte Mickelstrasse.
32.	5. 1.45	Abwehr Hochkopf/Lothringen.
33.	6. 1.45	Abwehr ostw. Hochberg/Lothr.
34.	7. 1.45	Abgew.Feindangriff m.Pz.-Unterst.nördl.Strasse Wildenguth-Puchstal.
35.	8. 1.45	" " " "
36.	9. 1.45	" " " "
37.	10. 1.45	" " " "
38.	11. 1.45	" " " "
39.	15. 1.45	Abwehr Höhe nördl. Schwarzenberg/Lothr.
40.	18. 1.45	Abwehr u.teilweise Vernichtung eines Stosstrupps.
41.	19. 1.45	Abwehr Höhe nördl. Schwarzenberg/Lothr.
42.	13. 3.45	Abwehr nordwestl. Hagenau-Saar(ostw.Hagenau/Saar).
43.	14. 3.45	" " "
44.	15. 3.45	Abwehr und Sicherung der Absetzung 1,2 km nördl. Britterhof.
45.	16. 3.45	Abwehr bei Losheim u. Durchbruch durch den Einschliessungsring.
46.	31. 3.45	Abwehr am. Angriffe mit Pz.-Unterstützung bei Hösbach.
47.	1. 4.45	Abwehr eines am. Angriffs mit Pz.-Unterstützung südl. Rohrbrunn.
48.	2. 4.45	Abgewehrter Angriff mit Pz.-Unterstützung und Gegenangriff bei Rodenbach.
49.	5. 4.45	Abwehr eines am. Angriffs mit Pz.-Unterstützung bei Rümpa.
50.	11. 4.45	Abwehr eines am. Angriffs mit Pz.-Unterstützung bei Wundelshausen und Falkenstein.

H-Sturmbannführer

Nahkampf-tage	Tag	Ort nach Regimentsbefehl	Bescheinigung des Kompanieführers
1.	1.7.4	Inf.-Werk Salla.	
2.		Angriff bei km 23.	
3.	3.11.4	Angriff bei km 14,2.	
4.	8.11.4	Angriff bei km 14,5.	
5.	.11.4	Spähtrupp Hau-wara.	
6.	.11.4	Angriff auf Nau-wara.	
7.	7.5.42	Angriff See 73.	
8.		Spähtrupp km 23.	
9.		Spähtrupp Nau-wara.	
10.	12.11.4	Abwehr See 75.	
11.	22.5.42	Angriff Kampfgruppe Schreiber.	
12.	22.5.42	Stosstrupp auf fdl. Bunkerlinien.	
13.	.5.42	Angriff See 75.	
14.	.5.42	Abwehr bei Kampfgruppe Jordt.	
15.	.5.42	Gegenstoss See 75/74.	

Nahkampf-tage	Tag	Ort nach Regimentsbefehl	Bescheinigung des Kompanieführers
15		Nahkampftage gem. Btl.-Befehl vom 10.11.43 anerkannt. Nahkampfspange 1 Stufe mit Wirkung vom 19.3.44 verliehen.	SS-Oberstürmführer u. Adjutant
16.	30.6.43	Abwehr Mende-wara.	
17.	11.10.43	Stosstruppunternehmen 1000 m westl. Mende-wa...	
18.	7.5.44	Abwehr Landzunge Kapa...	SS-Oberstürmführer u. Adjutant

2338. Dm A 6. 2 Ag. Heidelberger Gutenberg-Druckerei GmbH. 4135 · V. 43

₭-Ostuf.

Nah-kampf-tage	Tag	Ort nach Regimentsbefehl	Bescheinigung des Kompanieführers
19.	12.7.44	Angriff Tungohügel.	
20.	15.7.44	Einbruch Schneiserhöhe	
21.	17.7.44	Angriff Tungohügel.	
22.	1.8.44	Abgew.Angriff zw.1.Kp und Abscn.Perflinger	
23.	14.9.44	Feindangriff ostw.der Korja-Strasse.	
24.	16.9.44	Abgew.Verstoss ostw. Km 14 der Korja-str.	
25.		Verteidigung Kemi	
26.	8.10.44	Verteidigung u.Absetz aus Kemi	
27.	9.10.44	Jagdtruppgef.Kojula.	
28.	9.10.44	Abgew.Feindangriff km 41,9 alte Nickelstr.	
29.	12.10.44	Angriff bis km 41.	
30.	14.10.44	Abgew.Feindangriff km 41,4 alte Nickelstr.	
31.	18.10.44	Abgew.Feindangriff km Nickelstr.	

Nah-kampf-tage	Tag	Ort nach Regimentsbefehl	Bescheinigung des Kompanieführers
32.	5.1.45	Abgew.Angr.	
33.			
34.			
35.			

2372. Dtn A.G.I.43F. Heidelberger Gutenberg-Druckerei G.m.b.H. 215 jV. 43

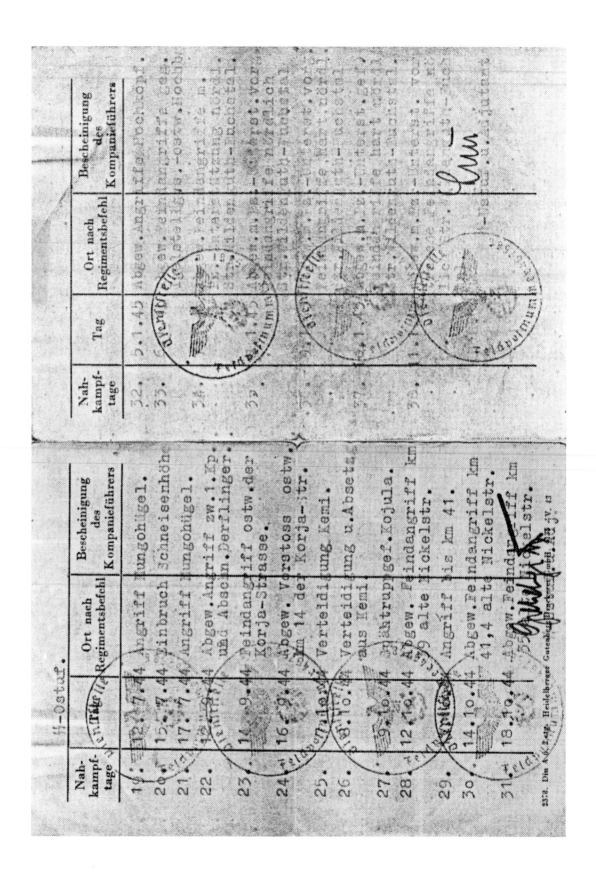

Nah-kampf-tage	Tage	Ort nach Rgts-Bef. Bescheinigung des Kp.-Führers
47.	1.4.45	Abwehr eines amerikanischen Angriffs mit Pz.-Unterstützung. südl. Rohrbrunn.
48	2.4.45	Abgewehrter Angriff mit Pz.-Unterstützung u. Gegenangriff bei Rodenbach.
49.	5.4.45	Abwehr eines amerikanischen Angriffs mit Pz.-Unterstützung vor ges. Abschnitt des Btl. bei Rümpa.
50	11.4.45	Abwehr eines amerikanischen Angriffs mit Pz.-Unterstützung vor ges. Abschnitt des Btl. bei Hundelshausen u. Falkenstein.

SS-Obersturmführer

Nah-kampf-tage	Tag	Ort nach Rgts-Bef. Bescheinigung des Kp.-Führers
39.	15.1.45	Abwehr Höhe nördl. Schwarzenberg/Lothr.
40.	18.1.45	Abwehr u. teilw.Vernichtg. eines Stosstrupps Höhe nördl. Schwarzenberg/Lothr.
41.	19.1.45	Abwehr Höhe nördl. Schwarzenberg/Lothr.
42.	13.3.45	Abwehr nordw. Bunker 382 (ostw. Hamm)
43.	14.3.45	Abwehr nordw. Bunker 387 (ostw. Hamm)
44.	15.3.45	Abwehr u. Sicherung der Absetzung 1,2 km nördl. Britterhof.
45.	16.3.45	Abwehr bei Losheim u. Durchbruch durch den Einschließungsring
46.	31.3.45	Abwehr amerikanischer Angriffe mit Pz.-Unterstützung vor gesamten Abschnitt des Btl. bei Möbbach.

SS-Obersturmführer.

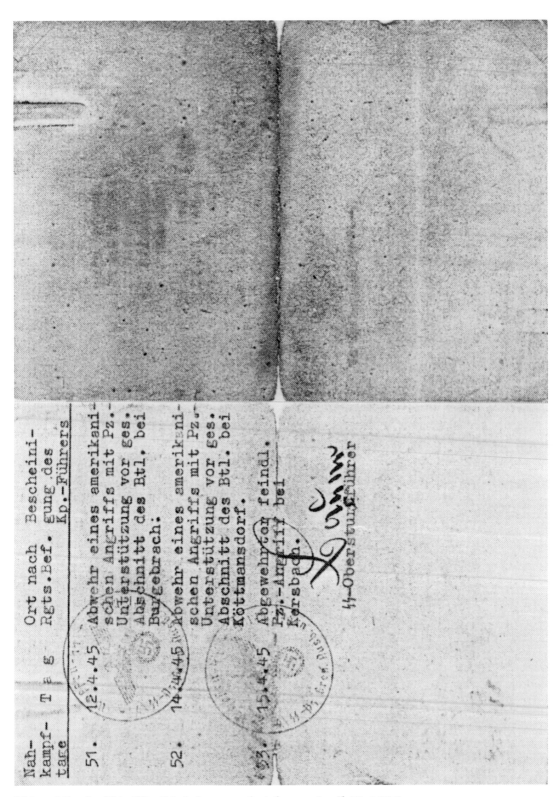

Nah- kampf- tage	Tag	Ort nach Rgts.Bef.	Bescheini- gung.des Kp.-Führers
51.	12.4.45	Abwehr eines amerikani- schen Angriffs mit Pz.- Unterstützung vor ges. Abschnitt des Btl. bei Burgebrach.	
52.	14.4.45	Abwehr eines amerikani- schen Angriffs mit Pz.- Unterstützung vor ges. Abschnitt des Btl. bei Köttmansdorf.	
53.	15.4.45	Abgewehrter feindl. Pz.-Angriff bei Kersbach.	⚡⚡-Obersturmführer

This soldier had his fifty-third close combat day on April 15, 1945.

BESITZZEUGNIS

DEM   ⫴-Obersturmführer

(DIENSTGRAD)

(VOR- UND FAMILIENNAME)

1./⫴-Schützen-Btl.(mot) 6

(TRUPPENTEIL)

VERLEIHE ICH FÜR TAPFERE TEILNAHME
AN 30 NAHKAMPFTAGEN

DIE II. STUFE DER
NAHKAMPFSPANGE

Im Felde, den 7.11.44

(ORT UND DATUM)

(UNTERSCHRIFT)

⫴-Hauptsturmführer
u. Bataillonsführer

(DIENSTGRAD UND DIENSTSTELLUNG)

**This Close Combat Clasp in Silver was awarded
three weeks after the thirtieth close combat day.**

BIBLIOGRAPHY

Allgemeine Heeresmitteilungen
1942, No. 1030
1943, No. 66, 114, 115
1944, No. 174, 443, 511

War Diary, Regimental Group 258 of February 1-8, 1944

Douglas, Gregory, "The Nahkampfspange", in: *The Military Advisor,* Winter 1991-92.

Michaelis, Rolf, *Die Verwundetenabzeichen 1918-1936-1939*, Erlangen 1995.

Michaelis, Rolf, *Die Sturmabzeichen des Heeres*, Erlangen 1996.

Michaelis, Rolf, *Die Nahkampfspange des Heeres*, Erlangen 1996.

Rudloff, Gerhard, "Die Nahkampfspange des Heeres", in OMJ No.38, Freiburg 1981.

Rudloff, Gerhard, "Das Weisse im Auge des egners", in Jörg M. Hormann, *Die Uniformen Der Infanterie 1919 bis heute*, Friedberg 1989.

OTHER BOOKS BY ROLF MICHAELIS

SS-Heimwehr Danzig in Poland 1939

SS-Fallschirmjäger-Bataillon 500/600

The 10th SS-Panzer-Division "Frundsberg"

The 11th SS-Freiwilligen-Panzer-Grenadier-Division "Nordland"

The 32nd SS-Freiwilligen-Grenadier-Division: "30.Januar"

Combat Operations of the German Ordnungspolizei,
1939-1945: Polizei-Bataillone • SS-Polizei-Regimenter

Cavalry Divisions of the Waffen-SS

Panzergrenadier Divisions of the Waffen-SS

The Kaminski Brigade

Belgians in the Waffen-SS

The German Sniper Badge 1944-1945

The German Tank Destruction Badge in World War II

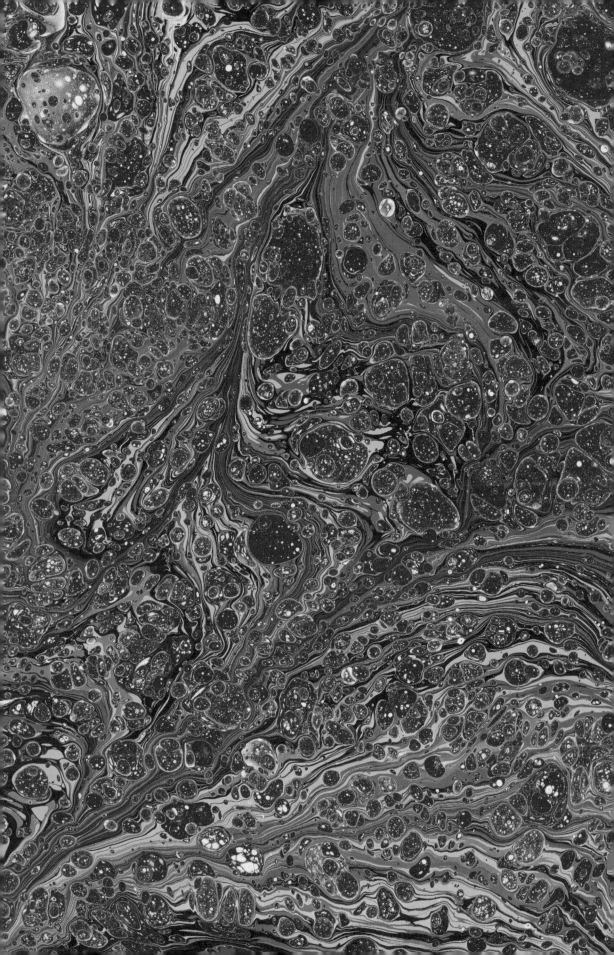